TIGHNABRUAICH

Steamer services to the Kyles of Bute

by

Ian McCrorie

The Tighnabruaich Pier Association

© Ian McCrorie
2002

Published by
The
Tighnabruaich
Pier Association
in co-operation
with The
Douglas Press
Glendaruel
Argyll PA22 3AE
Tel:
01369 820229

ISBN
1 902831 82 9

Printed by
Cordfall Ltd
Glasgow
G21 2QA

Sands dry at low Water

Cross Section F.C.H.

Front cover:
Turbine steamer
Queen Mary II
*lying at the pier
in an idyllic
summer
afternoon in the
late 1950s*

*A plan of
Tighnabruaich
Pier dating from
the mid-
nineteenth
century*

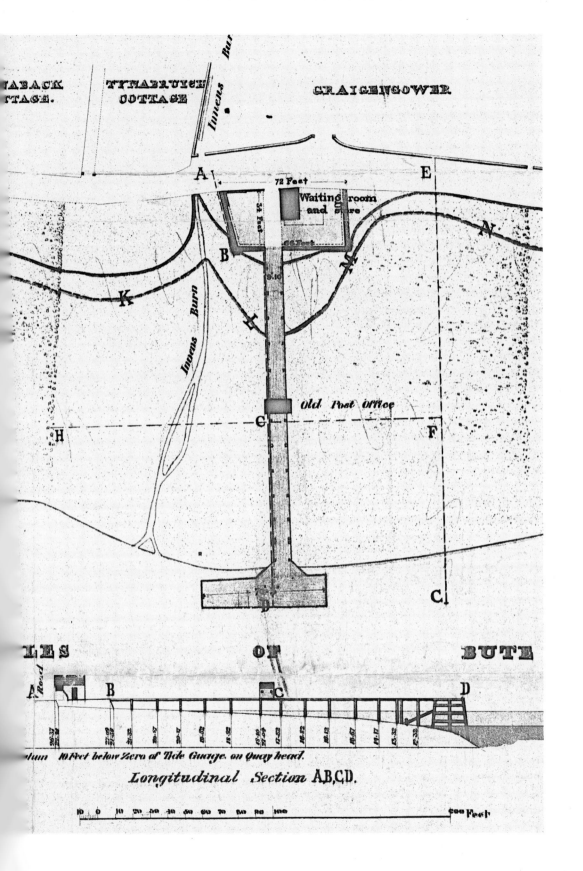

CRAIGENGOWER

72 Feet

Waiting room and store

N

A

B

K

Innens Barn

M

L

Old Post Office

H G F

C

BUTE

Longitudinal Section A,B,C,D.

10 Feet below Zero of Tide Guage on Quay head.

The Ivanhoe *in the Kyles of Bute*

Early days

IT IS IRONIC THAT ONE OF THE VERY FEW TRADITIONAL PIERS LEFT ON THE FIRTH OF CLYDE HAS ORIGINS LOST IN THE MISTS OF TIME. The best estimate for the construction of the Tighnabruaich 'wharf', as it was known at the time, is the mid-1830s. It was built for the Castle Steam Packet Company, formed in 1831–2, the first fleet of Clyde steamers which acted together to ensure that a regular service could be guaranteed with ships which were interchangeable. The first steamship to sail through the Kyles of Bute was the *Dumbarton Castle* on her way from Glasgow to Inverary in July 1815, her first season and less than three years after the sailing of the first ever Clyde steamer *Comet* in August 1812. At that time only the 'house on the hill' from which the village was to take its name was in existence: if passengers or cargo had to be embarked or disembarked a rowing boat would come out to the little wooden paddle steamer as there was no quay big enough for her to tie up. With road transport virtually non-existent any communication had to be by sea.

When the original wharf was constructed two ships put in regularly, one en route from Glasgow to Inverary calling in the late morning while the other sailed in the opposite direction calling in the early afternoon. Their progress was leisurely, cargo being more important than passengers. The ships most likely to be seen would be the *Inverary Castle* [sic] (1820), replaced in 1836 by the *Tarbert Castle*, and the *Dunoon Castle* (1826). In 1838 a rival appeared in the *Argyle*: the Castle Company's honour was at stake. The fledgling company responded by selling the *Tarbert Castle* and building a new, faster and more substantial ship of the same name. Sadly she was wrecked the following January but her machinery was salvaged and used to power a new *Inverary Castle (1839)*, probably the best known of the Castle fleet. She survived for fifty years, seldom deviating from her original route through the Kyles to Inverary.

1839 was a very significant year in the development of sailings to and from Tighnabruaich. Messrs Thomson & McConnell,

owners of a coastal steamer fleet, entered the trade by placing a so-called 'swift steamer' in summer on the run between Glasgow and Ardrishaig where connection could be made via the Crinan Canal with the network of steamers operating in the West Highlands. The interests of passengers became paramount and, originally operating only three days a week, the steamer offered a day excursion from Glasgow for the first time, admittedly at the somewhat unearthly hour of 0500 from the Broomielaw. The paddler's name was *Brenda*, replaced in 1840 by the *Shandon*.

Paramount among steamship owners of the time were Messrs J & G Burns. It was in 1846 that they took over ownership of the Castle Company and, being on friendly terms with Thomson & McConnell, they were able to place their new crack steamer *Dunrobin Castle* on the 'swift steamer' service through the Kyles to Ardrishaig, by now, incidentally, calling in addition at Tarbert for the Islay connection. Next year the route received a huge boost when Queen Victoria and Prince Albert sailed through the Crinan Canal both going to and returning from their tour of the Highlands—thereafter it was called the Royal Route. That year the Clyde run was maintained by the *Rothsay Castle* [sic] and later the *Cardiff Castle* while in 1848 the *Pioneer* took over. She was a new recruit to the fleet, having been built for a Greenock Railway associate who had sold out to Messrs Burns; she was in turn replaced by the 'crack' steamer *Merlin* in 1850.

When the Castle Company sold their fleet the wharf at Tighnabruaich came into the hands of one Arthur Scoular and it remained in the ownership of his family for the next hundred years. His great grandson, Alan Millar, is at the start of the twenty-first century one of the guiding lights behind the campaign to save the pier for future generations. At the time there were two calls in each direction each day, the swift steamer berthing twice and the 'cargo boats', usually the *Inverary Castle* and *Dunoon Castle*, calling once to or from Greenock and Glasgow.

Fishing boats at Tighnabruaich

Hutcheson's second Iona—a model in Greenock's McLean museum

Royal Route and Royal Mail

A MATERIAL CHANGE OCCURRED ON 10 FEBRUARY 1851 FOR ON THAT DATE A NEW FIRM TOOK OVER THE OPERATION OF THE BURNS' WEST HIGHLAND FLEET. This was David Hutcheson & Co., with one David MacBrayne, a nephew of the Messrs Burns, as junior partner. Mr Hutcheson had been all but running the operation on behalf of his master, but now he did so on his own account. The *Pioneer* again became a familiar sight as she called twice daily at Tighnabruaich wharf or quay, to be replaced in 1852 by a fine two funnelled steamer *Mountaineer*, which was reputedly the fastest steamship in Europe—at 15 knots on trial. The Royal Route was the only Clyde service to be taken over by Hutcheson—the Loch Fyne cargo run was now operated by the Glasgow & Loch Fyne Steam Packet Company using the two existing steamers. The Loch Fyne herring trade, however, demanded a third ship and the new company bought the sturdy Stornoway steamer *Mary Jane* and in 1852 replaced the ageing *Dunoon Castle* by the larger *Duke of Argyll*. The Kyles residents, used for many years to the austere black funnels, relieved by a white band near the top, of the Castle Steamers, now saw the red and black of the Hutcheson fleet and the red white and black, rather like the *Waverley* of today, of the Loch Fyne steamers. At this period, of course, there were few adequate roads and the steamship was the recognised mode of travel. 1857 saw the takeover by David Hutcheson & Company of the three Loch Fyne steamers: the *Duke·of Argyll* was replaced by the *Dolphin*, which had formerly sailed out of Oban, but it was not long before two ships sufficed, the *Inverary Castle* and *Mary Jane*.

In 1855, a new and speedy *Rothesay Castle* was placed on a 'spoiling' run through the Kyles to Tarbert and Ardrishaig but she only lasted for one season. That very year, the first Iona took up service in place of the *Mountaineer*—she was reputed to be the fastest steamship in the world. In fact, with her new oscillating engines, she was at least two knots faster than her predecessor. In the same year, a vitally important event occurred when David Hutcheson & Company was awarded its first mail contract: from then on the Hutcheson steamers always carried the mail to Tighnabruaich. In the following year, however, an equally significant event occurred. A twin-bowed craft called the *Sir Colin Campbell* opened for the first time a packet service from the Kyles to Glasgow, returning in the evening. By now substantial feuing had been taking place round the shores of the Kyles and such a venture was reckoned to be economic. Although she only lasted for one year her mantle was taken over by others like the *Eagle* (1852) and the summer 'commuter' run was here to stay. At the same time the *Mail*, a new steamer that year, commenced a daily summer service from Glasgow to the Kyles of Bute. It is no coincidence that Kames, a mile or two down the West Kyle from Tighnabruaich and the home of a Gunpowder Mill since 1839, had a steamboat pier erected in the same year: the packet boat now lay there overnight. Ormidale Pier in Loch Riddon opened in July 1856 and Colintraive Pier, in the East Kyle, was built around the same time. For many years one of the packet steamers

Two Williamson paddlers Sultana (left) and Viceroy off Greenock racing for the coast

The 1864 Iona at Tighnabruaich (Mr McKechnie's Tighnabruaich series)

Captain McLean's Marquis of Bute at Auchenlochan Pier

used to lie over the weekend at Ormidale, locally known as the "Cuckoo's Nest". Sometimes the ship would be careened at the top of the loch for cleaning; on certain Sundays she would play host to the local minister who conducted a church service aboard.

In 1862 Captain Alexander Williamson entered the field of steamboat operations when he bought the 'handy little flush-decked steamer' *Sultan*, which had spent her first year on the Kilmun station. He was to become very closely associated with the Kyles of Bute trade for the next thirty years. The *Sultan* and her two consorts *Sultana* (1868), reputedly the greatest of all Clyde steamers at manoeuvring at piers, and *Viceroy* (1875) were essentially the only vessels plying to the Kyles other than the Royal Route 'swift steamers' and the Loch Fyne cargo boats. They were aptly called the 'Turkish fleet'. They were considered among the most reliable Clyde steamers, never grabbing the headlines, but earning a steady income for their cautious owner.

Meanwhile in America the Confederates were looking for fast ships to run the Yankee blockade—and they had to search no further than the Clyde and West Highlands. The *Iona* was sold at the end of the 1862 season (but did not get further than Gourock Bay where she was sunk) and her successor, the second *Iona*, similarly was sold west in 1863: she reached Lambay Island off Dublin before she too foundered. The third *Iona*—the famous one—entered service on Thursday 23 June 1864 to start off a magnificent career of 72 years. She inherited her predecessor's deck saloons and furnishings and was altogether the foremost Clyde steamer of her day—in contrast to the Kyles piers' other callers, Williamson's *Sultan* and the cargo boats *Inverary Castle* and *Mary Jane*. In winter only the last two called, giving Tighnabruaich and the other piers one daily service in each direction, but from 1869 the 'swift steamer' sailed throughout the year, albeit from Greenock rather than Glasgow. The *Iona* was altogether too grand a ship for winter work and she was replaced by the *Chevalier* (1866) or *Mountaineer*.

Late that same year the Glasgow & South Western Railway commenced a service from Glasgow to Prince's Pier in Greenock; the company soon made a special arrangement with Captain Williamson to provide rail connections with his steamers from Rothesay and the Kyles. Once the full pattern of sailings was established the *Sultana* was usually to be found on the daily excursion from Prince's Pier shortly after ten o'clock, known as the Midday Kyles run. For almost thirty years prior to the opening of the new terminus Greenock Steamboat, or Customhouse, Quay had been the main railhead via the Caledonian network. In 1865 a railhead at Wemyss Bay had opened and a short-lived and ultimately unsuccessful service commenced from and to Kames and Tighnabruaich with a paddler appropriately named *Kyles*. The following year the North British Railway, having gained a foothold to the Clyde Coast at the North Bank town of Helensburgh, had put into action an ambitious plan to run a service with their *Meg Merrilies* to the Kyles and Ardrishaig but this was also an ignominious failure.

Little change took place for the best part of a decade, except that the Loch Fyne herring trade was declining rather badly with the introduction of smart screw steamers by the fish merchants and it was

SKIPNESS PIER 242

C.S. 120. Kames Pier and the Kyles.

The cargo steamer **Minard Castle** *at Skipness Pier in Kintyre*

found possible to withdraw the *Mary Jane* from the Inveraray run in 1875. [She subsequently was considerably altered and upgraded, re-appearing as the *Glencoe*.] For seven years the *Inveraray Castle* [sic] alone catered for the cargo needs of the communities in the Kyles and Loch Fyne but in 1882 a group of local merchants, feeling the service was inadequate, formed the Lochfyne & Glasgow Steam Packet Company Limited, built the graceful black-funnelled screw steamer *Minard Castle* and placed her on the Glasgow–Kyles–Inveraray run in opposition.

A much more serious challenge to the Hutcheson steamers, however, had appeared in 1877 in the form of the *Lord of the Isles*. Sporting her funnel colouring of red with black top and two white stripes associated with the company trading to Lochgoilhead, she rudely shattered the monopoly of the excursion trade to the Kyles of Bute and Loch Fyne by introducing a day cruise, for the first time ever, all the way to Inveraray. She was the best equipped tourist steamer on the river and took quite a proportion of the *Iona*'s traffic. Hutcheson's reply was to build the famous *Columba*, which made her maiden voyage the following year. Being the fastest, longest and most lavishly furnished vessel on the firth the *Columba* was able easily to eclipse her rival. Tighnabruaich Pier now had at least nine regular daily calls in summer—two from the *Columba*, two from the *"Lord"*, at least four from Williamson's steamers and one daily from the *Inveraray Castle*. The *Iona* was found other work (at Oban from 1880) and now normally only appeared on the Royal Route in the spring and autumn. A year later, in 1879, the final Kyles of Bute Pier was constructed. This was the iron pier at Auchenlochan, just over a mile south of Tighnabruaich. Auchenlochan did not feature as extensively in the steamer companies' timetables and calls were largely confined to Williamson's railway connection steamers and the cargo boats. In 1879 too MacBrayne, by now the sole partner of David Hutcheson & Company, decided to carry on the business of the company in his own name, simply as David MacBrayne.

A further two-funnelled crack paddle steamer made her debut in 1880. This was the *Ivanhoe*, owned by the Firth of Clyde Steam Packet Company and skippered by Captain James Williamson, eldest son of Captain Alex. She was unique in three ways—her colour scheme (with her two all yellow funnels) and the naval uniforms of her crew led many to think she resembled a private yacht rather than a river steamer, she started her day not from Glasgow but from Helensburgh and, most important of all, she was run on temperance principles. She introduced the famous Arran via Kyles excursion to the firth and instantly became very popular, her patrons being able to circumvent the 'teetotal' restriction by taking on board the ubiquitous 'Ivanhoe flask'... Tighnabruaich had another daily caller.

By 1884, Tighnabruaich, now fifty years old and in fact a veteran among Clyde piers, was so run-down that it had to be completely rebuilt. According to the contemporary press: "Greenheart piles are to be used and the pier itself is to be longer and somewhat broader than the present one, but the gangway leading to the pier and the offices are to be the same. The work will be carried out in sections, so that traffic may be

The second **Lord of the Isles** *approaches Kames Pier*

An atmospheric shot of the great Columba alongside Tighnabruaich

Two Victorian ladies pose at Auchenlochan Pier with the special excursion steamer Victoria alongside

carried on without interruption." The work took place between 1 October 1884 and 1 February 1885. At this period there was no way of regulating the arrival of steamers approaching the pier at the same time and as ships were becoming ever larger and faster accidents were not unknown. A new system of pier signalling was embodied in the Clyde Navigation Act of 1887 and Tighnabruaich pier, along with the others in the river, was given a signalling tower in 1889. This familiar landmark was to last for almost a century.

Meanwhile in 1885 David MacBrayne commissioned a very attractive two-funnelled paddle steamer *Grenadier*. Although primarily built for the excursion trade out of Oban she appeared almost every winter on the Ardrishaig run, thus calling at Tighnabruaich. The following year Captain Alex Williamson had the temerity to invade MacBrayne territory and berth his Kyles packet steamer, often the *Viceroy*, at Ardrishaig over the weekend. In retaliation, with the *Grenadier* now safely ensconced at Oban, MacBrayne was able to return the *Iona* to the Clyde and for almost twenty years she would leave Ardrishaig every morning at a quarter to six and sail, via Tighnabruaich, to the Broomielaw, returning at half past one. At the other end of the spectrum, the veteran *Inveraray Castle*, doyen of the fleet, was unfit for further service and was withdrawn after the 1890 season. The paddle steamer *Cygnus*, herself 36 years old, was bought in from Weymouth to replace her but she was too unwieldy for the run and chartering of little screw cargo vessels became the order of the day. One such steamer, the *Aggie*, was so closely associated with the run that she actually appeared in the company's fleet list.

Railway competition

IT WAS CAPTAIN JAMES WILLIAMSON OF THE *IVANHOE* WHO BECAME MARINE SUPERINTENDENT OF THE CALEDONIAN RAILWAY IN 1888 and who the following year found himself in charge of a new fleet working out of a new railhead at Gourock, some three miles nearer the coast resorts than Greenock, Prince's Pier. The ships were soon registered in the name of The Caledonian Steam Packet Company. The private steamers running in connection with the G&SW Railway were soon eclipsed at almost every turn: almost, as the new company made very little impact on the Kyles of Bute trade. Inevitably the "Sou'-West" fought back and in 1891 were given Parliamentary permission to own their own steamers. Captain Alex Williamson, brother of Captain James, was appointed Marine Superintendent. One of the first results was that the Railway Company bought over the Turkish fleet, Captain Alex having died the previous year. The ships serving the Kyles were soon sporting the new very pretty colour scheme of grey hulls and red and black funnels rather than the old and rather drab black and white. Much more important was the commissioning of new tonnage, obviously a top priority. Twins appeared early on, the *Neptune* and *Mercury*, and in 1892 the first sister replaced the old *Sultana* on the main runs to and from the Kyles; but it was the second, the *Mercury*,

P.S. "Waverley" at

which was to form a close relationship with all five of the Kyles piers. Berthing overnight at Kames and over the Sabbath at Ormidale, she sailed in the morning for Prince's Pier and returned around one o'clock on her day excursion and then in the evening with the regular travellers who commuted daily to the city. A further Sou'-West service was offered to the Kyles piers from Greenock in the afternoon; various steamers were allocated to the route—largely the *Viceroy* from 1892 until 1895 and then one of the 1893 sisters *Glen Rosa* or *Minerva* for the following six years.

At this time, therefore, Tighnabruaich would receive fifteen calls daily—one from each of the two cargo steamers, four from the *Mercury* and two from the afternoon steamer on the railway connection service, one from the *Ivanhoe* on her way to Arran, two each from the *Columba* and *Iona* on the Royal Route and two from the *Lord of the Isles*. The "*Lord*", incidentally, had been sold to the Thames in 1890 and replaced by a new build of the same name, larger and with the now customary deck saloons the full width of the hull. The next expansion came in 1894 when the G&SW placed the *Neptune* on a spoiling run against the *Ivanhoe* with her Caley connections from Prince's Pier to Arran via the Kyles: she put in at Tighnabruaich on her outward journey. The *Neptune* only remained on this route for two seasons, as in 1896 the company's latest flier, the *Jupiter*, took over. By the 1897 season the *Ivanhoe* had been bought over by the CSP (and fitted with a bar) and placed on general excursion sailings. Her position on the Arran route was taken by the favourite steamer *Duchess of Rothesay* (1895): competition was at white heat but Captain James was to admit that the traffic carried by the two steamers was less than the *Ivanhoe* carried by herself in her heyday. The following year, 1898, saw further calls at Tighnabruaich. While the two south bank railway companies were tussling for supremacy, the North British Steam Packet Company, operating out of Craigendoran, was muscling in on the act, with a fair degree of success. The Kyles did not feature prominently in its schedules until 1898 when one of its crack paddle steamers, the *Redgauntlet*, was placed on an excursion round Bute, sailing anti-clockwise. On her outward journey she was rostered to put in at the pier, day excursion passengers returning by MacBrayne's as far as Rothesay and picking up the NB boat there. The grander *Waverley* superseded the *Redgauntlet* in her first season, 1899, but it was usually the *Redgauntlet* which performed the Round Bute trip. NB expansion continued in 1902 when one of their ferry-class paddlers, the *Dandie Dinmont*, was scheduled for an afternoon cruise to the Kyles, calling at the various piers and turning at Kames.

The other newcomer in 1898 was the twin-funnelled paddle steamer *Galatea* (1889). That year the Caley Company for the first time had decided to compete directly with the Sou'-West for a share of the excursion market to the Kyles piers by placing one of their fleet on a service from Gourock almost duplicating the *Mercury*'s from Prince's Pier. They increased their presence the following year when the other 1889 paddler *Caledonia* ran an afternoon trip from Gourock to mirror the *Glen Rosa* or *Minerva* from the G&SW terminal.

Dear Tigh-na-Bruaich Pier   4/8/04   Kyles of Bute

We are having a very jolly time so far, + have been
several trips. Arran is nothing to this, the water + think in
time will take to the little boats, we have seen nothing yet to
beat Tighnabruaich, so glad we came. Your with love — J.P.

Stengel's postcard of the Sou'-West steamer **Mercury** *or* **Neptune** *at Tighnabruaich*

A truly revolutionary steamer appeared on the Clyde in 1901. This was the first commercial ship in the world powered by steam turbines— the *King Edward*, operated by yet another son of Captain Alex Williamson, Captain John. In 1902 she was placed on a service to Tarbert and Ardrishaig and for the third time MacBrayne had to respond. The *Columba* delayed her return voyage by some 90 minutes and the *Iona* was given a very demanding schedule involving two double runs between Ardrishaig, Wemyss Bay and Prince's Pier, calling on all but the morning express down run at Tighnabruaich. Meanwhile the winter boat *Grenadier* was brought back to the Clyde for the summer and offered a daily service from Kames and the other Kyles piers to the Broomielaw and back. This extravagance, which gave Tighnabruaich a further three calls daily, could not last and in 1904, apart from the Glasgow Fair fortnight, the *Grenadier* returned to Oban, although the *Iona* remained on her hectic roster.

Arguably 1903 was the 'high noon' of sailings to and from Tighnabruaich. MacBrayne provided seven passenger calls daily, the G&SW railway connection steamers six and the CSP four while the *Jupiter* and *Duchess of Rothesay* each called en route to Arran and the *Lord of the Isles* to and from Inveraray. The ships of the North British Steam Packet Company had meanwhile been taken into the direct ownership of the parent railway company: retrenchment followed and the calls were now limited to one daily by the *Waverley* which had been placed on the Round Bute excursion. Captain John Williamson, of Turbine Steamers Ltd., also owned two white-funnelled paddle steamers, the *Benmore* and *Strathmore*, and one of them during the summer and occasionally in winter offered a service from the Kyles to Glasgow as much for cargo as passengers. With the *Minard Castle* and MacBrayne cargo boat also touching at the pier the number of daily calls was as high as 28. In addition the Sou'-West's flier *Juno* (1898) called fairly frequently at one on the Kyles piers in her role of Ayr Excursion steamer; there were numerous special excursions while ships in most fleets offered evening cruises which were becoming ever more popular.

The Sou'-West paddler **Mars** *leaving Kames Pier*

Changes to the railway fleets took place almost annually in the early years of the new century. In 1902 the new G&SW steamer *Mars* took her place along with her older sisters on the afternoon Kyles run; this arrangement lasted only for four years as in 1906 the *Neptune* returned to this roster and remained on it. Meanwhile, also in 1902, the *Caledonia* was demoted to the Holy Loch run and her place on the opposition afternoon Kyles station taken by the *Marchioness of Lorne* (1891), while the following year the new *Duchess of Fife*, destined to be one of the most popular Clyde steamers of her day, took over on the Midday Kyles roster from the ageing *Galatea*. By the late 1900s, however, the railway companies were beginning to reap the consequences of years of extravagance and in 1908 remedial action started to be taken as units were withdrawn from service. In 1909 a pooling arrangement, by necessity, came into in force. The Caley immediately withdrew their two steamers from the Kyles runs, leaving the railway connections entirely in the hands of the Sou'-West twins *Neptune* and *Mercury*, and

the prestigious Arran via Kyles excursion was pooled. The plan was that in any year one company would provide the Arran via Kyles sailing and the other the 'lifeline' service to Arran from Ardrossan. Thus in 1909 the CSP provided the Prince's Pier–Gourock–Arran sailing with their former Ardrossan–Arran steamer *Duchess of Hamilton* (1890); in 1910 the *Jupiter* was on the run; in 1911 the Caley turbine *Duchess of Argyll* (1906); in 1912 the Sou'-West flier *Glen Sannox*; in 1913 the *Duchess of Rothesay* in July and *Duchess of Argyll* in August; and in 1914 once again the *Jupiter*.

Calls at Tighnabruaich in the 1909 season would have been cut to a daily total of only nineteen if it had not been for one further change. After the turbine *King Edward* had successfully inaugurated her Ardrishaig excursion in 1902 she extended her sphere of operation to Inveraray in the following season, in opposition to the *Lord of the Isles*. The fat was really in the fire when she from 1909 was diverted to sail not round Garroch Head but rather through the Kyles, thus affording direct competition—and providing Tighnabruaich with two additional calls. The *"Lord"* only lasted for four years till she gave up the uneven struggle: she was, rather incongruously, taken over by Turbine Steamers Ltd. and placed on a cruise round Bute.

Kames Pier with the CSP's **Marchioness of Lorne**

The Great War and its aftermath

IT WAS NOT UNTIL THE OUTBREAK OF THE GREAT WAR IN AUGUST 1914 THAT THIS SETTLED PATTERN CHANGED. Early in 1915 the first group of the Clyde passenger ships was requisitioned for war service and a Shipping Controller, under Admiralty restrictions, was appointed to oversee a joint steamer service on the firth. Later it was discovered that paddlers, with their shallow draft, made excellent minesweepers and soon nearly all of the pleasure steamers were transferred to the white ensign. Further difficulties arose from the closing of an anti-submarine boom between Dunoon and Cloch Point, thus effectively partitioning Clyde services. The Kyles communities, still with no effective access by road, depended almost entirely on the sea for their transport links and so a skeleton service had to be provided even in the darkest days of the war. In 1915 and 1916 the G&SW continued to provide an overnight and midday run, but from their Ayrshire railhead of Fairlie. In 1915 too, John Williamson's paddler *Kylemore* (1897), the *Strathmore*'s successor, even gave a service from Wemyss Bay en route to Inveraray. From 1917, however, the CSP supplied the link, at least in summer, and the railhead changed to the more convenient Wemyss Bay, but as all the company's ships had been requisitioned, chartered vessels had to be brought in, often veterans of the MacBrayne or white-funnelled fleet. MacBrayne's themselves continued to provide the Royal Mail steamer on the long-established Ardrishaig run, albeit from Wemyss Bay and not the Upper Firth. The *Iona* was the mainstay in 1915 and most of 1916 but when she was chartered by the CSP the *Columba* had to take over at the height of the season. MacBrayne vessels introducing themselves to Tighnabruaich at this time, either on the

Spencer's photograph of the pioneer turbine **King Edward** *approaching Tighnabruaich*

The **Lord of the Isles** *arriving at Tighnabruaich*

T S "Queen Al...

A Spencer photograph of the second **Queen Alexandra** at Tighnabruaich

Royal Route or under charter, included the *Fusilier* (1888), *Gael* (1867) and *Mountaineer* (1910).

The war was also the cause of a change in the workings of the cargo sailings on the Clyde. At the request of the Admiralty, Clyde Cargo Steamers Ltd. was formed in August 1915 to provide a minimum service to the outlying Clyde ports. The interests of MacBrayne, John Williamson and the Minard Castle Shipping Company were amalgamated, together with Messrs Hill and Company which provided various cargo services with their vessel *Bute 4*. Before this date MacBrayne had usually allocated one of two passenger and cargo vessels to the trade, the *Cygnet* or *Fingal* (1878), together with the cargo carrier *Texa* (1884). On the appearance of the *Cygnet* in 1904 a daily departure from Glasgow to the Kyles and Loch Fyne had been reintroduced after an absence of about thirty years: this meant that with the *Minard Castle* in opposition there were now three daily cargo calls at the Kyles piers. As all the interests were now merged, this provision was cut from 1915 to two, normally the *Bute 4* and *Minard Castle*. Incidentally, the *Minard Castle* ran aground late in 1918 and the relief steamer employed was none other than the *Glencoe* , the old *Mary Jane* renamed.

Although the conflict ended in November 1918, it was many months before the Clyde returned to any semblance of normality. With many ships lost in the war, it was still a much watered-down service which was offered compared with pre-war days. The first sign of the return to the old routine came on 1 February 1919 when the boom was lifted and the *Chevalier*, on the Royal Route, immediately reverted to Prince's Pier and Gourock rather than Wemyss Bay. The first railway steamer from Prince's Pier was the chartered *Isle of Cumbrae* (1884) which reinstated the Midday Kyles run from 1 April. When the summer timetable commenced on 1 June the *"Cumbrae"* changed to the Afternoon Kyles roster and her place on the main service was taken by the *Juno*. The overnight run was reintroduced at the same time: surely the *Juno* must have been the largest and grandest steamer ever to berth overnight at Kames Pier. The Caley colours were also seen every morning at Tighnabruaich when the turbine *Duchess of Argyll* took up the Arran via Kyles roster, in abeyance since 1914. Finally the *Lord of the Isles* returned to excursion sailings, but she was now restricted to a daily run from Glasgow to Tighnabruaich. During the 1919 season, then, calls at Tighnabruaich Pier stood at ten, plus the two visits from the cargo boats. The *Juno*, incidentally, was only on the Kyles roster for one year: in 1920 the *Mercury* returned to her old haunts and remained on the station for some years. The afternoon Kyles roster, however, was given only on Saturdays from 1920, and was normally taken by the *Jupiter*.

1920 saw the return of the Inveraray excursion by a turbine, but on most days it was not the *King Edward* but her consort the *Queen Alexandra* (1912) which carried out the sailing for the next few years. The white and black funnels associated with John Williamson were also seen quite frequently when the paddler *Queen-Empress* (1912) called; between 1920 and 1929 she was employed on a varied programme of excursions from coast towns, often to one or more of the Kyles piers. The red, white and black funnels of the North British

The Ayr Excursion steamer **Juno** in her tricolour funnel colours at Ormidale

The **Duchess of Rothesay** *in LMS colours at Auchenlochan*

were not normally seen in the Kyles during this period; it was 1924 before a Craigendoran steamer regularly ventured through the Narrows. The *Kenilworth* (1898) or *Talisman* (1896) was that year placed on an early afternoon run to Tighnabruaich. By now the NB had become part of the London & North Eastern Railway Company (LNER) just as the Caledonian and G&SW had been absorbed in the London, Midland & Scottish Railway (LMS). It had been obvious since the days of pooling followed by the Great War that the railway companies would one day merge: the Act of Parliament bringing this about took effect from 1 January 1923. After two years when the funnels of the South Bank steamers were seen as an amalgam of the two former rivals, the LMS adopted the standard yellow and black funnel. Little change in service was evident though the combined fleet continued to use each other's railheads and Prince's Pier gradually succumbed to the supremacy of Gourock. The morning and evening Kyles runs, however, ceased to be the preserve solely of the *Mercury*. The two Caley railway connection steamers *Duchess of Fife* and *Duchess of Rothesay* took their turn berthing overnight at Kames. In 1926 in fact the *"Rothesay"* was promoted to the Midday Kyles roster, the *Mercury* taking her place out of Rothesay and Dunoon.

Services were interrupted during the twenties by industrial unrest, culminating in the General Strike of 1926, but, despite this, a fine new steamer, with for the first time an enclosed upper deck and initially at least with revolutionary high pressure turbines, was built for the Inveraray excursion. The *King George V* appeared in September 1926 and remained on the station for the next nine years, although the larger *Queen Alexandra* usually returned for the Glasgow Fair fortnight each year. Another Clyde steamer reappeared in 1926. This was the *Marmion* (1906) which had been laid up after one post-war season; she replaced the *Talisman* or *Kenilworth* on the LNER Kyles roster. In 1926 also the LMS introduced a Sunday sailing for the first time not to Tighnabruaich but to Auchenlochan. The *Jupiter* and *Duchess of Rothesay* alternated on this roster and called en route round Bute. Passengers for Gourock on the return journey had to sail via Garroch Head. Five years on this excursion was advertised merely to the Kyles of Bute, the steamer turning at Auchenlochan while from 1933 the steamer also put in at Tighnabruaich.

A characteristic Spencer pose— white-funnelled turbine **King George V** *approaching Tighnabruaich*

The twenties ended sadly for aficionados of Clyde piers. By now road transport, both by omnibus and lorry, had advanced sufficiently that adjacent communities no longer needed to have separate piers and this trend could be clearly seen throughout the river and firth. Kames Pier was one of the first to succumb: it finally closed after the 1928 season. The previous year MacBrayne's had lost two of their oldest paddle steamers, the *Chevalier* by stranding while on the winter Ardrishaig run and the *Grenadier* by fire at Oban. The winter run on the Royal Route was affected: the slow and inadequate *Fusilier* was placed on the route until the company could be reconstituted and money made available for replacement tonnage. This came in the winter of 1931/32 when a revolutionary ship, the diesel-electric vessel *Lochfyne*, took her place on the winter station. A sharper contrast could hardly be imagined.

The LNER paddler **Marmion** *at Auchenlochan*

The officers throw stones in the water as the 1934 Mercury lies at Auchenlochan

R.M.S. COLUMBA AT TIGH

An atmospheric shot of the **Duchess of Hamilton** *leaving Tighnabruaich*

New ships for old routes

THE THIRTIES, DESPITE THE DEPRESSION, WAS AN EXCITING DECADE FOR THE STEAMER LOVER: the Clyde fleet was all but renewed and a second generation of railway steamers built. Initially the changes bypassed the Kyles piers, although in 1932 the palatial turbine steamer *Duchess of Hamilton* replaced the old LMS paddler *Juno* as Ayr excursion steamer and so put in fairly frequently. In 1934, however, twin paddle steamers *Caledonia* and *Mercury* appeared indirectly to replace the older vessels of the same name: they now alternated on the Sunday cruise to Tighnabruaich and Auchenlochan. More importantly the new *Mercury* was to be found on the Midday Kyles roster, displacing the *Duchess of Rothesay*, while the *Caledonia* supplanted the old *Jupiter* on the Saturday afternoon run.

Evening cruises have always formed an integral part of the Clyde excursion trade. Such cruises were in vogue as early as the 1850s but it was the *Ivanhoe* in the eighties which should receive the credit for starting regular runs from the railhead piers. Many were non-landing but for those offering time ashore one of the Kyles piers would be a favourite destination. Such cruises were at their height in the 1930s. On some occasions the steamers were chartered by students, usually with some ploy as an advertising gimmick. Sometimes the ruse was "to kill the Queen Midge" at Tighnabruaich; inevitably someone succeeded and the tiny beast was borne aloft for everyone to admire the bravery and prowess of its captor. There were three annual events which always attracted a fleet of steamers—Brodick Fair, Largs Fair and, most important of all, Rothesay Illuminations at the end of August. As far as the Kyles piers were concerned, the steamer berthing overnight would often take the evening cruise but on occasions an exchange of rosters would take place for traffic reasons; for example, back in the 1920s the Kyles steamer *Mercury* was needed to cope with the crowds from Largs while the smaller *Marchioness of Breadalbane* (1890) was perfectly adequate for the numbers offering from the Kyles.

During the 1935 season rumours spread that MacBrayne's two remaining veterans *Columba* and *Iona* were likely to be withdrawn for scrapping at the end of the summer. Sadly these rumours were substantiated and the two noble ships were indeed broken up the following year. Some weeks later their replacements became public knowledge. The combined fleets of the white-funnelled steamers were to be carved up, MacBrayne's receiving the two Turbine Steamers. The *King George V* was sent to Oban while the *Queen Alexandra* had a third funnel and mainmast added and her name changed, rather cleverly, to *Saint Columba*. In 1936 she took over the Clyde leg of the Royal Route, sailing daily from Glasgow at 0711 to Tarbert and Ardrishaig via Tighnabruaich. The goodwill of the Turbine Steamers trade, however, was invested in the CSP, part of the LMS empire. The *Duchess of Argyll* was allocated to the Inveraray station three days per week (and Campbeltown the other three weekdays). She thus continued to call at Tighnabruaich on Mondays, Wednesdays and Fridays while her newer and grander consort *Duchess of Montrose* (1930) sailed on the route

An aerial shot of the **Columba** *at* **Tighnabruaich Pier** *as* **Buchanan's Isle of Arran** *passes on her Kyles cruise from Glasgow*

25

The new LNER paddle vessel Talisman *with the cargo boat* Arran *at Auchenlochan*

Spencer frames
the Duchess of
Argyll *with trees as
she returns from
Tighnabruaich*

additionally on Thursdays. Meanwhile the new paddle steamer *Caledonia* was switched to the daily Arran via Kyles excursion, the *Mercury* took her place and the *Duchess of Rothesay* returned to work the Midday Kyles roster, the former white-funnelled paddler *Queen-Empress* rather surprisingly partnering the *"Fife"* on the basic roster involving the packet sailings from and to the Kyles.

The LNER ships also underwent change at this period. The old *Talisman* was withdrawn and replaced by an unconventional diesel electric paddle vessel of the same name. In 1935, her first season, she took over the Kyles run from the *Marmion* and remained on it for almost five seasons. The final substantial change in the thirties came in 1937 when two modern ferry class paddlers were built, happily perpetuating the names *Jupiter* and *Juno*. They were placed on the basic rosters which involved them in berthing overnight alternately at Rothesay or in the Kyles, at Auchenlochan on weeknights and Ormidale over the Sabbath. In 1939, then, the last season before the Second World War broke out, Tighnabruaich received only up to ten regular passenger calls per day. MacBrayne's *Saint Columba* called twice, the CSP/LMS fleet tied up eight times—in the morning and evening the *Jupiter* and *Juno*, around midday the *Duchess of Rothesay*, in the late morning the Arran steamer *Caledonia* and morning and late afternoon on most days the Inveraray steamer, usually *Duchess of Argyll*. On Saturday afternoons an additional LMS steamer would berth and on certain Sundays (since 1937) the Ardrossan–Arran steamer *Glen Sannox* even put in en route to and from Inveraray. The Sunday afternoon cruise from Gourock was also still on offer but the LNER that year only had three steamers in regular service and the Kyles piers did not figure in the ships' rosters. One must not of course forget the cargo steamer, by now the *Minard* (1926) or *Ardyne* (1928), the *Minard Castle* and *Bute 4* having been withdrawn.

Left: *Spencer
captures the new LMS
paddler* Juno *as she
nears Tighnabruaich
Pier on her evening
run*

*A rare shot of the
cargo boat* Ardyne
arriving at Kames Pier

The three-funnelled turbine Saint Columba *alongside at Tighnabruaich*

War again

FEW SERVICES SURVIVED THE SECOND WORLD WAR UNLESS THEY
WERE CONSIDERED ABSOLUTELY ESSENTIAL. Excursion sailings were
dropped and the railway companies all but ceased to run to the Kyles
piers for the duration of the conflict. The one exception occurred on
summer Sundays from 1941 when the turbine steamer *Marchioness of
Graham* offered a sail to Tighnabruaich from Millport, Largs and
Rothesay with the return journey at 1530 billed as a railway connection
service to Wemyss Bay by changing at Rothesay. The *Saint Columba's*
last ever run from Glasgow Bridge Wharf was on Monday 4 September
1939, the day after had been declared against Germany. Because of
the Cloch–Dunoon boom her terminus became Wemyss Bay. Her
sojourn there did not last long, however, as she was requisitioned as
the Boom Defence HQ in Greenock's East India Harbour. Three of
MacBrayne's new motor vessels of the thirties then maintained the
service—initially the Skye mail boat *Lochnevis* (1934) and from late
March 1940 the normal winter boat *Lochfyne*. She was relieved for her
annual refit by the Islay mail steamer *Lochiel* (1939) and then, after she
herself had been returned by the Admiralty in 1944, the *Lochnevis*
once again. As the MacBrayne steamer had never called at
Auchenlochan and Ormidale these two piers were closed to passenger
traffic for the six war years, and in fact Ormidale Pier never reopened.
The *Lochfyne* started using Gourock as her railhead from April 1946
but the *Saint Columba* was still 'called up' that first post-war summer
and the service was provided by the *King George V*—familiar territory
for her perhaps but with red rather than white funnels. It was not until
May 1947 that the *Saint Columba* reappeared. The "George",
incidentally, did not entirely forsake the Clyde: she was occasionally
rostered for the Tighnabruaich, Tarbert and Ardrishaig run in emergency
and later was even given some charter sailings.

The summer of 1946 saw the return of some excursion sailings,
although the fleet was a shadow of its pre-war self. The Arran via Kyles
run was revived on a daily basis, but given to the *Duchess of Montrose*.
The Inveraray excursion was reduced to thrice weekly with the *Duchess
of Hamilton* as the regular steamer and the *Duchess of Argyll* was
demoted to the Midday Kyles run, turning at Tighnabruaich and not
Auchenlochan. The pier at Colintraive, in a state of extreme disrepair,
was in use for that one post-war season; it was closed to the railway
steamers in August 1946 and to the MacGrayne's steamer *King George
V* on 5 October. From 16 December a ferry call was substituted but
that was short-lived: the *Saint Columba* brought the practice to an end
on 8 July 1947. The ferry class paddlers on the Rothesay station did not
call at any of the Kyles piers, except during the restricted service
operating in the spring and in late September. The last morning and
evening commuter run, then, had taken place in 1939. The
Craigendoran paddler, now usually the LNER flagship *Jeanie Deans*
(1931), still gave an afternoon trip to both Tighnabruaich and
Auchenlochan. Tighnabruaich was now purely a tourist destination,
apart from the all-year-round MacBrayne mail service. The Kyles

*Spencer notices a
rowing boat
witnessing the
arrival of the
Duchess of
Montrose at
Tighnabruaich*

Children play on the beach as the Jeanie Deans *approaches Tighnabruaich in her post-war guise—another Spencer photograph*

Millport steamer Duchess of Fife *in the Kyles of Bute*

community, however, did receive one substantial boost. For nearly a century there had been day excursions from the heart of Glasgow to Dunoon and Rothesay and many of these incorporated cruising in the afternoon. In 1946 for the first time the 1100 run from Bridge Wharf actually called at Tighnabruaich rather than merely cruising through the Narrows. The ship normally allocated to this service was the pioneer turbine *King Edward*, which had been such a prominent visitor in the years preceding the Great War, although then with white rather than yellow funnels. On Sundays for that year only the LNER rostered two steamers to touch at the Kyles piers—the *Jeanie Deans* and *Talisman* from Craigendoran—while Tighnabruaich continued to be the Sabbath destination of the Millport steamer, now the *Duchess of Fife*. She too had called extensively in a past life.

A rare photograph of the new Waverley *in her original LNER livery at Auchenlochan*

Nationalisation

CHANGES IN 1947 INCLUDED THE REAPPEARANCE OF THE *SAINT COLUMBA* ON THE ROYAL ROUTE, the revival of the Ayr excursion programme with the small turbine steamer *Marchioness of Graham* (1936), the cutting of the Inveraray sail to twice weekly, on Tuesdays and Thursdays only, and, most significantly as events turned out, the appearance of a new LNER paddle steamer, the *Waverley*, alternating with the *Talisman* on Sundays. 1948 witnessed more than one major alteration to the *status quo*. On 1 January the assets of all Britain's railways were vested in a new state authority called the British Transport Commission, trading under the name 'British Railways'. The full integration of the LMS and LNER fleets took years to come to fruition: the immediate effect was that all the Craigendoran paddlers had their funnels painted LMS yellow (strictly buff) and black. The year also saw the beginning of a long association of the *Duchess of Montrose* with Inveraray. Traffic considerations demanded that more sailings be given to Campbeltown and so the frequency of the Arran via Kyles excursion

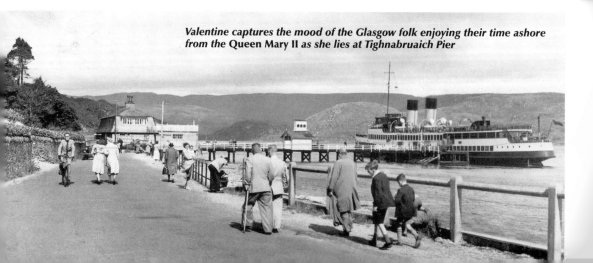

Valentine captures the mood of the Glasgow folk enjoying their time ashore from the Queen Mary II as she lies at Tighnabruaich Pier

The Jeanie Deans in her new BR colours at Auchenlochan in 1948

The paddle steamer Caledonia shares the East Kyle with yachts and other small craft

was reduced and the roster given to the *"Montrose"* to be performed on her non-Inveraray days. Only the LNER steamers were calling at Auchenlochan and they ceased to do so at the end of the season. Actually the *Waverley* had suffered a severe paddle fault while berthed at Auchenlochan on her Sunday cruise on 29 August; she was taken out of service and replaced by the *Talisman*, which therefore made the last call. The previous day had been Cowal Games Day and eyewitnesses claim that the veteran Craigendoran paddler *Lucy Ashton* (1888) actually made the Kyles calls on that occasion, possibly uniquely, when the fleet was overstretched. Finally in 1948 the cargo service, where loadings had been becoming sparser as time went on, was withdrawn from Tighnabruaich at the end of the year, road transport being substituted. In a sense this was the last remaining link with the opening of the pier over a century before. The last season of the decade saw the withdrawal of the Saturday Arran via Kyles run although rather bizarrely in that year the *"Montrose"* sailed on her normal timings as far as Tighnabruaich before returning to Gourock.

1950 witnessed the pier changing hands for the first time in over a century. The Tighnabruaich Estate, owned by Arthur Millar, grandson of the Arthur Scoular who had bought it in the 1840s, sold it to George Olding, the then piermaster. In 1950 too the Kyles excursion of the *Jeanie Deans* was transformed, to popular acclaim, into a Round Bute cruise, with a call at Tighnabruaich on the outward leg for two seasons only; the cruise was not offered on Saturdays. On what was arguably the busiest day of the week, Saturday, Tighnabruaich now had to make do with only three calls, the *Saint Columba* both ways and the *King Edward* from Glasgow Bridge Wharf. Weekdays, however, also suffered a cut with the permanent withdrawal of the age-old Midday Kyles run, which had been carrying fewer and fewer passengers. In the same year the paddler *Caledonia* replaced the turbine *Duchess of Montrose* on the Arran via Kyles run on Mondays and Fridays while the following year the now elderly *Duchess of Argyll*, in her last year in service, returned to the haunts of her youth by performing the roster on Fridays. In addition in 1951 the other veteran turbine, *King Edward*, exchanged duties in her last season with her younger and roomier consort *Queen Mary II* (1933). This happened because the 1100 Glasgow–Kyles run had become much more popular than the alternative, the 1000 to the Arran Coast: it marked the start of a long association between the *"Mary"* and Tighnabruaich Pier.

This was a time of deep change on the Clyde Coast. The war had taken its toll of the Clyde fleet and those which survived were not always the most economical vessels. Virtually all the steamers burned expensive coal as fuel, wage inflation was a force very much to be reckoned with and new safety measures were forcing up the cost of ships' maintenance. The ever increasing competition from road transport kept down revenues as did the changing habits of holidaymakers who were beginning to experience travel outside Scotland; the derationing of petrol in 1950 also had profound consequences. 1952, then, brought much-needed economies and two of the four major excursion vessels were by and large not given regular rosters—the subsequent cuts

The **Saint Columba** *desperately tries to overtake the* **Duchess of Montrose** *in the West Kyle*

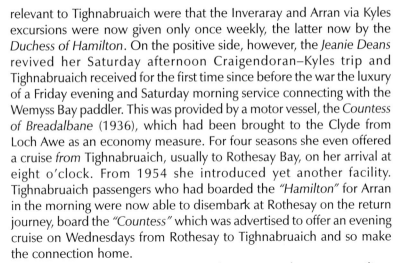

The motor vessel Countess of Breadalbane in her white-hulled condition down the side of Tighnabruaich Pier

relevant to Tighnabruaich were that the Inveraray and Arran via Kyles excursions were now given only once weekly, the latter now by the *Duchess of Hamilton*. On the positive side, however, the *Jeanie Deans* revived her Saturday afternoon Craigendoran–Kyles trip and Tighnabruaich received for the first time since before the war the luxury of a Friday evening and Saturday morning service connecting with the Wemyss Bay paddler. This was provided by a motor vessel, the *Countess of Breadalbane* (1936), which had been brought to the Clyde from Loch Awe as an economy measure. For four seasons she even offered a cruise *from* Tighnabruaich, usually to Rothesay Bay, on her arrival at eight o'clock. From 1954 she introduced yet another facility. Tighnabruaich passengers who had boarded the *"Hamilton"* for Arran in the morning were now able to disembark at Rothesay on the return journey, board the *"Countess"* which was advertised to offer an evening cruise on Wednesdays from Rothesay to Tighnabruaich and so make the connection home.

After a period of annual change, the pattern of excursion sailings established in 1953 held for a considerable period. This was the year when a quartette of new smallish diesel passenger vessels, the "Maids", made their appearance, although the only one to be rostered to sail to Tighnabruaich during the season was the *Maid of Skelmorlie*, which gave the weekend railway connection sailings (for that year only). They were used for certain basic services and short cruises round the firth while the established steamers concentrated on the long distance excursions. The Craigendoran-based *Maid of Argyll* (or other vessel) was often to be found on a new afternoon cruise to Tighnabruaich during the currency of the spring timetable in April and May from 1954. The Inveraray day trip by the *Duchess of Montrose* was restored in 1953 to twice weekly, on Tuesdays and Thursdays; the *"Hamilton"* continued on the Arran via Kyles roster on Wednesdays but this was supplemented by a Monday trip from Craigendoran by the *Waverley*. One of the features of the programme was the race which often ensued around 1100 from Rothesay to Tighnabruaich between the *"Duchess"* and the *Saint Columba*, the MacBrayne steamer and the *"Hamilton"* being particularly well-matched, and for brief moments the excitement of the pre-war days returned. The *Queen Mary II*, now the only steamer sailing regularly from Bridge Wharf, still called every afternoon while the *Jeanie Deans* continued to put in an appearance on Saturday afternoons. She and the *Waverley* shared the Sunday run, calling not long after the departure of the Millport steamer. The old *Duchess of Fife* had by now been withdrawn and her place at Millport in 1953 taken by the former Holy Loch paddle steamer *Marchioness of Lorne*. Her cruising speed of 12 knots, perfectly adequate in her former life, meant that passengers were lucky to arrive at the Kyles pier before the hour of departure. She only lasted a year: from 1954 the former Craigendoran paddler *Talisman* was allocated this duty.

The car ferry revolution came to the Clyde in 1954 with the commissioning of three dual-purpose vessels essentially for the service between Gourock and Dunoon and Wemyss Bay and Rothesay. Tighnabruaich was affected only indirectly. During the inevitable cascade

A calm spring day at Tighnabruaich with the new motor vessel Maid of Argyll alongside

MacBraynes' Diesel electric vessel **Lochfyne** *arriving at Tighnabruaich*

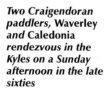

Two Craigendoran paddlers, **Waverley** *and* **Caledonia** *rendezvous in the Kyles on a Sunday afternoon in the late sixties*

of vessels the *Caledonia* became Ayr excursion steamer and so put in an appearance periodically. Revenues—and morale—increased and, encouraged by a period of splendid weather, the Clyde began to experience a post-war renaissance. For three years between 1955 and 1957, for example, the Sunday All-the-Way sailing was duplicated as required, often by the *Duchess of Montrose*.

By the end of the 1958 season the *Saint Columba*, now not far from her fiftieth birthday, was in urgent need of expensive boiler repairs and MacBrayne's had contrived to make the winter vessel *Lochfyne* available all the year round. On 27 September the Clyde's only three-funnelled turbine called at Tighnabruaich for the last time amid fond farewells. The *Lochfyne* indeed became the mainstay of the service, relieved for annual overhaul by her smaller consort *Lochnevis*. Without an adequate direct road the Kyles communities still had to rely on the sea route for mail and other essentials.

The paradigm established in 1953 had to be modified twelve years later. The heady days of the mid-fifties were a distant memory and a series of bad summers, together with spiralling staff costs and the decreasing appeal of the traditional Clyde holiday, had eroded the economic base of the railway steamers. For some years around this time the September turbine cruises were often taken by the more economical paddlers *Caledonia* and *Waverley*. The fleet, incidentally, was now marketed under the name of the registered owners, The Caledonian Steam Packet Company, rather than British Railways. A minor change occurred in 1962 when a "Maid", usually the "*Skelmorlie*", supplied the Wednesday evening connection. At the end of the 1964 season the *Duchess of Montrose* and *Jeanie Deans* were withdrawn and the cruise programme consequently curtailed. In her last four seasons, in a management attempt to equalise the working day, the "*Jeanie*" had alternated week about with the *Waverley* but now, spurred on by the drive for economy in the Beeching era, the CSP had to embrace retrenchment. The *Caledonia* was transferred to Craigendoran and the Ayr Excursion programme allowed to lapse. She now visited Tighnabruaich regularly on Mondays, en route to Arran, and on Saturday afternoons on her cruise from the Upper Firth. The *Duchess of Hamilton*, the last surviving cruise steamer from Gourock, called on Tuesdays bound for Inveraray and Wednesdays bound for Arran. The *Queen Mary II* was required for ferry work on Saturday mornings and so her Saturday cruise to Tighnabruaich, though probably carrying the heaviest load of the week, was axed. On Sundays the Kyles pier still had three visitors, the *Queen Mary II* from Glasgow, the *Talisman* from Millport and the *Waverley* from Craigendoran. The wee *Countess of Breadalbane* was now required full time as the Millport ferry: her Friday overnight run to Tighnabruaich was continued by the Rothesay-based pleasure cruiser *Maid of Bute* under charter, but this

arrangement was dropped after two seasons because of lack of traffic. One bright spot was the new colour scheme introduced for the CSP fleet in 1965: hulls were now painted 'monastral' blue and a red 'Caley' lion affixed to both sides of the yellow and black funnel.

It was on 13 October 1965 that the widow of the later piermaster

The **Duchess of Hamilton** *with her truncated masts calling at Tighnabruaich on her way back from Inveraray in her last season, 1970*

George Olding sold Tighnabruaich Pier to Argyll County Council—for the princely sum of £833 12s. 0d. (£833.60). The bargain included the pier lorry; it was agreed that George McBride would be confirmed as piermaster and that the shop at the head of the pier would be relet to the existing tenant. (For many years the shop housed Neil Angus's Licensed Grocers business.)

1966 brought about the withdrawal of the Millport vessel *Talisman* and her replacement by one of the four "Maids" on a four-week rota basis. On Sundays, however, the Tighnabruaich cruise from Millport was allocated to the *Waverley* with the *Caledonia*, her replacement on the run from Craigendoran, occupying the pier just as soon as she left. The *Queen Mary II* now cruised round Bute on Sundays and thus no longer put in an appearance.

The last turbine Queen Mary II negotiating the Narrows

The end of railway control

TWO EVENTS OF CRUCIAL SIGNIFICANCE OCCURRED IN 1969. Firstly, on 1 January, The Caledonian Steam Packet Company was wrested from railway control and became a wholly owned subsidiary of the bus-dominated Scottish Transport Group—with David MacBrayne Ltd following on 14 July. Secondly, the long-promised new direct road to the Kyles communities was opened so that there was now easy access to Dunoon, Colintraive and to Strachur and beyond, not least to Glasgow. These two happenings, directly or indirectly, proved to be the death knell of the mail service. On Tuesday 30 September the *Lochfyne*, dressed fore and aft on the outward journey, made her last sailing on MacBrayne's Clyde service. Part of the STG's policy was rationalisation of services and the CSP logically took over the run on 1 October. While the *Maid of Skelmorlie* was having mail lockers fitted to the alcoves outside her tearoom before she took up the run, the paddler *Caledonia*, rather uneconomically, was called in. As it happened this was also her last duty before she was withdrawn. The *"Skelmorlie"* took over and sailed continuously from 8 October until 14 February 1970 when the *Maid of Argyll* superseded her. On 29 May 1970, despite numerous representations, the all-year-round daily service from

The Maid of Cumbrae berthed at Tighnabruaich Pier while the King George V, on a charter cruise, lies off

Gourock came to an end. A substitute bus service carrying passengers, mails and parcels, was supplied between Tighnabruaich and Dunoon, with a connection from Rothesay by way of the Colintraive–Rhubodach ferry.

To make up for the loss of their daily steamer the Kyles communities in 1970 were offered a slightly increased cruise programme by way of a sop. This was the last season of the *Duchess of Hamilton* and she continued to perform the Inveraray and Arran via Kyles excursions. It was now the *Queen Mary II* which provided the Monday Arran cruise; the *Waverley* gave the Saturday and Sunday cruises from the Upper Firth but in addition on Fridays offered a special excursion to Tarbert and Ardrishaig via Tighnabruaich. Meanwhile the "Millport Maid" for two years performed her Tighnabruaich afternoon cruise on Mondays and Wednesdays as well as Sundays; for 1970 only a "Maid" also sailed to Ardrishaig on Wednesdays and Tarbert on Saturdays. No sailings were offered from Glasgow (Bridge Wharf). Without the *"Hamilton"* in 1971, the *Waverley* was allocated the Monday Arran via Kyles run and the *Queen Mary II* Inveraray and Wednesday Arran. This was the last year in which a "Maid" brought Arran passengers back to Tighnabruaich on Wednesday evenings in the course of an evening cruise. Clyde cruising continued its downward spiral in 1972: the only appearance of a "Maid" was the *"Argyll"* on the Sunday cruise from Millport. The *Queen Mary II*'s Arran cruise was now routed both ways via Tighnabruaich, thus affording a direct day excursion to and from the Kyles village. The *Waverley* no longer put in on Sundays and Mondays but she did touch at the pier on her way round Bute on Wednesday afternoons.

A momentous change took place on 1 January 1973. The Caledonian Steam Packet Company Ltd was renamed Caledonian MacBrayne Ltd (CalMac for short) and took over the combined shipping services of the CSP and David MacBrayne Ltd. The new company's undertaking was to provide lifeline services to the various islands and peninsulas in the West coast of Scotland. Cruising was an optional extra: a reduction in scope was inevitable. In 1973 Tighnabruaich still managed at least one daily call, except on Sundays. The two remaining steamers still put in four days per week but in addition called on the other days during their Round Bute Cruise. Craigendoran pier had now closed and the Saturday cruise was rerouted via Largs. After the absence of three years the red funnel had returned, now with a yellow disc and red rampant lion on each side. The CSP blue hulls had already been repainted the more traditional black following the demise of railway control in 1969.

1973 was the one and only year in which CalMac operated the *Waverley*. On 30 September the last sea-going paddle steamer in the world gave what was reckoned to be her final sailing but two months later it was announced that she was to be gifted to the Paddle Steamer Preservation Society, which had expended great efforts in the previous few years to market her unique appeal. Her future contribution to the Tighnabruaich story is detailed below. Meanwhile in 1974 and 1975 the *Queen Mary II* continued on the Arran excursion on Wednesdays and cruised to Tighnabruaich on Mondays and Saturdays. Great efforts

The CalMac paddle steamer Waverley *at Tighnabruaich in 1973*

The Waverley *and* Queen Mary II *pass in the Kyles*

CalMac cruise "steamer" Keppel *rests at Tighnabruaich*

The second generation car ferry Jupiter, *still with GOUROCK–DUNOON FERRY on her side, alongside Tighnabruaich*

were being made to publicise her as a fast, spacious turbine steamer; in 1976 the "*II*" was dropped from her name, she returned to Glasgow for her Monday Kyles cruise and even offered Friday and Saturday nostalgic specials but economics ruled otherwise and she was reluctantly withdrawn after 1977. Her place was taken by the dual purpose vessel *Glen Sannox* (1957) which had been refurbished for her new role as cruise steamer midweek and car ferry during busy weekends. She bravely tried to play her part for the next four years, continuing the Arran via Kyles excursion on Wednesdays and offering a Tighnabruaich cruise on Mondays (Tuesdays in 1980). In a last desperate attempt to keep the concept alive she was rostered to perform "Inter Resort Sailings" in 1981. Tighnabruaich was the destination on Tuesdays, Wednesdays and Fridays but there were no longer cruises *from* the pier. The "*Sannox*" fared no better and was inevitably withdrawn from her role as an excursion 'steamer'.

CalMac ships did not touch at Tighnabruaich between 1982 and 1984 but in 1985 help came form an unexpected quarter. During the middle of the day in July and early August the car ferry *Jupiter* (1974) was rostered to sail from Gourock, Dunoon, Wemyss Bay and Rothesay twice per week: her destination on Thursdays was Tighnabruaich. This arrangement only lasted for one year as another, admittedly smaller and slower, vessel was available for 1986. The *Keppel* (1961) had spent some twenty years as the Largs–Millport passenger ferry but this route was axed at the end of June. Her redundancy was turned to good use as she became at the height of the season a full-time CalMac Clyde cruise vessel. For the following eight summers she fulfilled her task fairly adequately, being especially popular with senior citizens for whom speed was not an issue. On three days per week (four in 1992) she sailed to Tighnabruaich and on Fridays from 1989 even offered a cruise into Loch Riddon from the Kyles pier. Once again, however, the economic argument reigned supreme and she was withdrawn after the 1992 season. (In fact she was sold and appeared in 1993 disguised as the blue-funnelled *Clyde Rose*; she advertised Tighnabruaich as her destination on three days per week. The whole venture, however, was abortive.) The *Jupiter* came to the rescue again in 1993 when she re-introduced inter-resort sailings, heading for Tighnabruaich on Tuesdays and Thursdays—and Wednesdays from July. CalMac charged particularly advantageous prices for pensioners this time round and loadings, if not the resulting revenue, were quite high. 1994 saw the three estuarial car ferries, known as 'streakers' because of their exceptional manoeuvrability, take their turn week about on the cruise roster. Tighnabruaich thus welcomed not just the *Jupiter* but also the *Juno* (1974) and *Saturn* (1977) on two days per week. In 1999 calls were extended to thrice weekly, but after the 2000 season, with CalMac concentrating purely on sailings within the undertaking with the Scottish Executive, the facility was withdrawn completely. The *Juno* made the last call on 22 September.

Tighnabruaich, however, did receive other calls. The Clyde Marine Motoring Company Ltd., founded by A D Munro of Greenock, owned several small motor vessels use largely for tendering and charter work.

Dual-purpose cruise vessel **Glen Sannox** *makes dramatic waves after sailing through the Narrows*

The preserved paddle steamer **Waverley** *lies at Tighnabruaich while* **The Second Snark** *awaits a berth*

The company's foremost vessel, *The Second Snark* (1936), was acquired in 1969 and in 1987 instituted a programme of cruises round the Firth at the height of the season. From 1990 destinations included Tighnabruaich once per week although from 1993 she sailed through the Narrows to the Kyles pier on at least two occasions weekly. Her passenger complement was obviously smaller than the CalMac vessels but nevertheless she performed a very useful function for a sector of the tourist market. Her consort was the *Rover* (1964) and she relieved each year from time to time; in fact in 1991 she was Clyde Marine's main cruise vessel and in 1993 she was given her own roster and sailed to Tighnabruaich most Fridays from Millport in her own right. The launch *Fencer* most unusually took the service twice in 2000. Meanwhile Clyde Marine in 1999 bought the larger *Poole Scene* (1974) and employed her on cruises with special parties to various destinations, including Tighnabruaich. In 2001, incidentally, she was renamed *Cruiser*.

The future is *Waverley*

THE MAIN USER OF TIGHNABRUAICH AT THE START OF THE THIRD MILLENNIUM IS THE *WAVERLEY*. The historic paddle steamer, last of the line, was laid up during 1974. In August of that year CalMac kept their word and she was 'sold' for a pound to the Paddle Steamer Preservation Society. The tacit assumption was that the paddler would be preserved statically but thanks to a monumental effort on the part of the enthusiasts and their professional advisers enough money was raised to repair her, drydock her and return her to steam. Her 'maiden' voyage under her new owners occurred on 22 May 1975, her first call at Tighnabruaich was on a chartered sailing on the 31st of the month while from the end of June she commenced her first of many summers sailing publicly on the Clyde. At weekends she was based in Glasgow and during the week at Ayr. She berthed at Tighnabruaich on Tuesdays en route from Ayr to Tarbert. Strikingly, her funnels had been repainted in the original LNER colours she had sported in 1947. Helped by the fact that she was essentially run by volunteers, she became the focus of a great deal of nostalgia and folk flocked to see her and to sail on her. Owned by Waverley Steam Navigation Company the operating concern became Waverley Excursions Ltd.

It took six years before the *Waverley* settled down to a pattern of sailings which changed little from season to season. In 1976 her Tighnabruaich and Tarbert day was changed to Monday while the following year she started making Tighnabruaich the destination of her "Doon the Watter" trip from Glasgow on Saturdays. In 1979 her Saturday trip became a non-landing cruise up Loch Riddon but the Kyles pier was restored next year. In 1980 also the Ayr–Loch Fyne trip settled on a Tuesday and that pattern of two calls every Tuesday and one on Saturday has continued till the present day, though for three years from 1986 she also made Tighnabruaich the destination of a trip from Ayr on Thursdays.

Other vessels associated with the *Waverley* have touched at

Waverley consort Balmoral at Ormidale on an enthusiasts' charter

Waverley consort Southsea makes a rare call at Tighnabruaich

Tighnabruaich Pier over the years. On 15 July 1977 the paddler tragically hit the Gantocks while manoeuvring into position to take Dunoon Pier. Fortunately she was refloated and, at great and unaffordable expense repaired. To keep the cash flowing her management chartered a motor vessel which had been transporting workers between Rothesay and an oil rig construction yard at Ardyne on the Cowal coast. The *Queen of Scots* was quickly painted in Waverley colours and sailed until the paddler returned at the end of August; although rather slower, she was able to perform a modified programme quite satisfactorily. She too called at Tighnabruaich on Mondays and Saturdays. Bought by another private firm, BB Shipping (Dunoon) Ltd., the following year, and sporting a yellow and black funnel, she attempted to muscle in on the Clyde cruising market, sailing to Tighnabruaich on Fridays in 1978 and Tuesdays in 1979. She was distinctly unsuccessful and eventually ceased plying when a writ was nailed to her mast.

Waverley Excursions were advised that a consort to the paddler could help to provide much-needed funds to keep her sailing. To this end a consortium bought the former Southern Railway vessel *Shanklin*, a spacious diesel vessel able to carry 1000 passengers, and brought her to the Clyde late in 1980. Renamed *Prince Ivanhoe* (a nice touch since 1980 was the centenary year of the old 'teetotal' boat *Ivanhoe*), she sailed for a fortnight in the early summer of 1981 on the *Waverley's* roster and thus visited Tighnabruaich on Tuesdays and Saturdays. That August, while sailing in the Bristol Channel, she struck a submerged object, had to be beached and was found to be beyond repair—a sad end to a fine ship. A successor was found in 1985 in the shape of MV *Balmoral* (1947), formerly of the Solent and Bristol Channel, at the time lying idle in Dundee. She too was taken in hand (though not to the extent of having her funnel painted red, white and black) and by the Glasgow Autumn Holiday Saturday of the following year she was able to put in her first appearance at Tighnabruaich. Apart from four years the *Balmoral* has closed the Kyles season each September Holiday Sunday, or since 1990, Monday. In 1987 the company had chartered the Sealink ferry *Southsea*, a quasi-sister of the *Shanklin*, to perform the Clyde sailings in September, in 1991 the *Waverley* needed urgent repairs and the *Balmoral* had to deputise for her in the Bristol Channel, while in 1992 and 1996 the *Waverley* closed the season herself.

Meanwhile the actual structure which was Tighnabruaich Pier soldiered on. Although piles had been renewed through the years it was over a hundred years since the last rebuild and time had taken its toll. The signalling tower, being redundant, was removed in 1980 but the construction substantially remained the same. It has remained in public ownership since 1965—Argyll County Council, Strathclyde Regional Council and now Argyll & Bute Council. Towards the end of the twentieth century some community-minded residents of the village realised that action was needed if the pier were to remain open. They formed The Tighnabruaich Pier Association and in November 1999 concluded a formal Partnership Agreement with the new local authority, Argyll and Bute Council, with a commitment to examine ways of conserving and possibly developing the pier.

Summer bliss on the upper deck of the Waverley as she approaches the Narrows